Fyne.

Lacus

aft

Lamprey=
stone.

Newcaft.

Twomey.

Banney fiu.

Ba=
ne.

MacYlym

Glan
yboy.

shotte.

Colerranne

ryan
ferty

Alexander

Dunlys=
the.

Carogh. Rush

Skyrres of
port Rush

furst

Glanarmo

Corane.

Racklyn

Portmuf
Knokfergus
is of

Maydens

Stone otter

A Book of Ireland

A Book of

IRELAND

Edited by Maureen Sullivan

Ariel Books

♣

Andrews and McMeel
Kansas City

Frontispiece: Lakeside Cottages by Paul Henry

ISBN: 0-8362-1066-2

The text of this book was set in Evangel and the display in Mearschaum. Book design and typesetting by JUDITH STAGNITTO ABBATE

CONTENTS

Contents

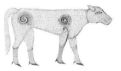

INTRODUCTION

A HUNDRED THOUSAND welcomes," is the saying proclaimed all over Ireland, where hospitality and friendliness are counted among the greatest of virtues. This remote, romantic island is a place of endless enchantments, from the soft, glowing beauty of the magical country-side with its famous "forty shades of green" to the bustling life of the towns. And everywhere there are reminders of Ireland's rich history: ivy-clad castles, tombs older than the pyramids, and ancient steep-roofed churches.

It is also a land rich in imagination. Close your eyes and it is easy to conjure up figures from the past: hooded monks sprinting across the turf with a troop of Viking warriors close behind; bards playing the harp while spinning tales of wonder; minstrels making music as lords and ladies dance. It is no surprise,

then, that the Irish are legendary storytellers. This land, steeped in superstition and folklore handed down through generation after generation, is alive with fairies, ghosts, banshees, and leprechauns with their crocks of gold.

Time is one of the greatest luxuries of Ireland, where people believe that "life is for the living" and will happily travel miles for a "craic," the Irish term for a rousing good time. Above all, the Irish like to enjoy themselves. Along with gambling, Guinness, and religion, horses and horse racing are major preoccupations of the Irish. So is the pub culture. Even the smallest town has innumerable pubs open all hours of the day and night, providing the social heart of the community, where a visitor is immediately made to feel welcome and can have a pot of tea, a simple, wholesome meal, or share in a round at the bar.

Many of the charms of Ireland are perfectly straightforward, but much of its real beauty is found along the back roads, where half-forgotten places breathe an air of suspended wonder. It is a land of richness and incongruities, where frequent, almost daily, rain showers also bring a glowing rainbow. Perhaps that reflects the true spirit of Ireland: a land of secret, smiling mystery.

AS EVERY IRISH schoolchild knows, there are no snakes in Ireland. According to tradition, they were banished by Saint Patrick, but in fact the land was too cold and too far north for snakes. But a rich variety of wildlife abounds in Ireland, including some species that are now very rare in Britain.

Otters and mink thrive in the many streams and rivers, sometimes setting up residence close to towns. There are pine martens in the forest parks, but this predator is rarely seen, coming out only at night to hunt small rodents. Seals and rare birds, including puffins, thrive on the many coastal waterways, and giant skate and basking sharks find shelter in the sea inlets and narrow straits along Ireland's rocky coast. Patient seawatching from a western headland may also be rewarded with a sighting of a school of dolphins or porpoises or the occasional whale feeding in the rich inshore waters.

Originally Ireland was densely covered with trees. Native species include the hawthorn, considered to be sacred, and the ash, used for making hurley sticks, for the traditional Irish sport of hurling.

The midlands and west of Ireland are covered with a number of small lakes and reed-fringed marshes. As a result, breeding water birds are extremely common and every waterway has its resident pair of swans, moorhens, and herons.

Limestone grassland, a special feature of the west of Ireland, is best exemplified by the Burren area in North Clare. It's a harsh place, bleak and gray, and can come as a surprise to those who think Ireland is always green. Its main attractions are a wealth of wildflowers, which include a mixture of Arctic, alpine, and Mediterranean strains (ferns, orchids, mountain avens), and the large amount of barren stone, whose cracks and fissures give shelter to the delicate plants. County Clare is also where you'll find the Cliffs of Moher. At their highest they tower 660 feet above the Atlantic Ocean. These sheer, ravaged crags of shale and sandstone are constantly being battered and eroded by huge waves.

The highest mountains in Ireland, Macgillicuddy's Reeks, loom above three spectacular lakes in Killarney, County Kerry. The lower slopes of the mountains are covered with what is often virgin forest, a surprise in a country that has cut down almost all its trees. Oak predominates, but you'll also find bilberry, woodrush, woodsorrel, and the famous arbutus, or strawberry tree, so called for its bright red (but inedible) fruit.

Soaring cliffs, rolling misty moors, white sandy beaches, and sparkling, twisting lakes: Ireland's beautiful scenery is breathtaking in its unspoiled and natural state.

THE BOGLANDS

LARGE PORTIONS of the lowlands in central Ireland are covered with peat bogs. Composed of dead grass or moss, these wetlands can be deceptively dangerous: pools of water, often forty feet deep or more, may be disguised by soft mats of vegetation on the surface. If you start to sink while walking on the bogs, don't struggle: wait until you're in deep enough to swim. Hand-cut peat has been the chief source of fuel for many centuries, due to the shortage of timber, coal, and natural gas in Ireland. About one-quarter of Ireland's electricity comes from this source.

Since mechanical cutting began in 1946, the boglands have been greatly diminished. Only recently have the Irish perceived the great importance of these natural ecosystems. Not only are the bogs home to rare plants, from mosses to bilberries, but they provide a habitat for birds. The peat gases also act as preservatives, and the bogs of Ireland have yielded rich archaeological finds (some of them almost a thousand years old): gold and silver artifacts, dugout canoes, and even human bodies.

THE GARDENS OF IRELAND

IRELAND IS KNOWN for its walled gardens, which are often found on the great estates. The high stone walls provide privacy as well as protection from wind and storms. At the same time, they

retain heat from the sun, making it possible to grow a wide variety of plants. Furthermore, the typical Irish "soft day" of gentle rain and sunshine is ideal for vegetation; many rare and tender species thrive in the subtropical weather. As a result, some of the loveliest gardens in the world exist as hidden treasures in this country.

Castlewellan Forest Park, County Down, includes the Annesley Gardens, enclosed by a wall and embellished by two fountains. The famous Mount Stewart Gardens, also in County Down, feature plants from all over the world, including Tasmanian Blue Gum trees. The Irish Agricultural Museum, County Wexford, contains some splendid examples of walled gardens as well as over two hundred species of trees and shrubs, ornamental lakes and hothouses. In County Wicklow, the Powerscourt estate is well-known for roses and flowering shrubs, an extensive range of conifers, gorgeous old eucalyptus and beech trees, a sitka spruce said to be Ireland's tallest tree, several walled gardens, a pet cemetery, and a Japanese garden.

Irish Whiskey and Beer

IRISH-GROWN and roasted barley is still the key ingredient in Ireland's famous Guinness stout, a rich, chocolate-looking brew topped with a thick, creamy head. Known variously as "the dark stuff," "the blonde in the black skirt," or simply, "I'll have a pint, please," Guinness stout was first brewed in 1759 in a factory along Dublin's Liffey River and quickly became the city's staple beverage. Guinness is served with ceremony. "Pulling a pint" is the high skill of the bar trade. The glass must be at a precise angle, the flow halted at an exact point, topping-up completed carefully. So be patient!

Irish whiskey, which Queen Elizabeth II once called her only true Irish friend, is also made from barley and is sweeter and more stinging than Scotch whiskey. The word "whiskey" comes from the Gaelic phrase, *uisge beath*, meaning "water of life." It can be served hot and spiced with lemon, cloves, and brown sugar. It can be served in the world-famous Irish coffee; the Irish version of eggnog, with brandy, beaten egg, milk, and lemon-ade; and in other ways too numerous to mention. Nevertheless, whatever the choice of drink, the truth is that the real draw of the local pub is talk. Traditionally, the Irish don't even keep alcohol at home except at Christmas; they go to the "local" to meet friends and exchange stories, gossip, troubles, humor, and wit.

♣ IRISH COFFEE

1 teaspoon sugar
1 serving strong black coffee
1 tablespoon heavy cream
generous measure of Irish whiskey

Dissolve the sugar in a long-stemmed, warm whiskey glass partially filled with coffee. Add whiskey to within one inch of the rim and stir. Hold a teaspoon upside down over the liquid, then gently pour the cream over the rounded part of the spoon so that the cream floats on the surface. Do not stir; drink the coffee through the cold cream.

A SHORT HISTORY OF IRELAND

T HE HISTORY of Ireland dates back to prehistoric times, and the countryside is dotted with remnants of that age: huge stone tombs, massive stone circles (at least one of which is thought to have been used to determine the shortest day of the year), and single standing stones, which may have marked graves.

The Celts began to invade Ireland about 700 B.C. An Indo-European group who had spread from central Europe southward into

Italy and Spain and westward through France and Britain into Ireland, the Celts were hospitable people who loved feasting, music, and storytelling. Celtic settlements took the form of ringforts, each with its own king. It is hard to separate the truth about the Celts from the stories they told about themselves; Irish folklore is full of Celtic myths.

Saint Patrick imported Christianity to Ireland in A.D. 432, challenging the high kings and druids and converting many to Christianity. Then, beginning in 795, pirate raiders from Scandinavia began attacking Ireland's shores, and some decided to stay. These Vikings caused grisly suffering, but eventually they settled into peaceful ways, often intermarrying and assimilating into the culture.

The Anglo-Normans of England, under Henry II, conquered Ireland in 1171, initiating 750 years of British domination. Monasteries flourished, and many great churches and abbeys were built under Anglo-Norman rule, including Cormac's Chapel at Cashel, County Tipperary, and Ballintubber Abbey, County Mayo, where mass has been celebrated continually for more than seven centuries.

Queen Elizabeth I (1533—1603) hoped to establish an English colony in Ireland; this began the English practice of "planting" Protestants in Catholic Ireland. Oliver Cromwell, following his victories in England, arrived in Ireland in the mid-1600s to conquer the Catholics by confiscating property from native Irish owners and setting up Englishmen in their place. The bloody battles that followed left Protestants in power and Catholics dead or banished to the remotest and poorest areas of the island.

Support in England grew for the legislative coupling of Britain and Ireland and the dissolution of the Dublin parliament. In 1801 Ireland was officially made part of Britain when the British Parliament passed the Act of Union. Ireland itself was now a land of utterly divided people: a minority Protestant ruling class and a politically powerless Catholic majority.

In 1845 a fungus wiped out the main food source, potatoes. This led to the great famine, which lasted until 1851. During those six years at least one million people starved to death, and another million emigrated to Canada, Britain, Australia, New Zealand, and the United States. The long-standing bitterness between the English and the Irish only deepened as a result: British government failed to intervene, and the absentee English landlords in particular continued to profit from exorbitant rents while remaining ignorant of, or indifferent to, the suffering of their tenants.

On Easter Monday, 1916, the Irish Republican Army (IRA) staged the Easter Rebellion to protest British conscription of Irishmen for their military forces in The Great War. The IRA was built on the philosophy of "Sinn Fein" (meaning "We, Ourselves") first expounded in 1898 by Arthur Griffith, a Dublin printer who founded a newspaper called the *United Irishman*. The rebellion was bungled when a shipment of arms was intercepted; undeterred, Padraig Pearse led the uprising anyway. After five days of firefights in downtown Dublin, the Easter rebels were captured and, according to British martial law, executed. The public mood in Ireland was sympathetic to the martyrs and, as a result, deeply anti-British.

In 1920 the British government was ready to seek a compromise that would keep Ireland within the British Empire but make concessions to Irish nationalism. A new Government of Ireland Act provided for a measure of home rule to be exercised by two parliaments in Ireland. In the general election that followed, unopposed Sinn Fein candidates took all but four seats in Southern Ireland.

In 1922, after protracted discussions and threats to resume hostilities in Ireland, weary delegates agreed to a treaty providing for an Irish Free State with dominion status. This allowed the six Ulster counties of Northern Ireland to remain within the United Kingdom, which includes Britain, Scotland, Wales, and Northern Ireland. The twenty-six counties of Southern Ireland further distanced themselves by becoming the Republic of Ireland in 1949 and ceasing to be a part of the British Commonwealth. The Free State,

named Eire, is governed by a bicameral parliament with a president and a prime minister.

THE IRISH LANGUAGE

ALTHOUGH ENGLISH is the main language of Ireland, it is spoken with an unmistakable Irish flair and lilt. This accent provides one of the most musical varieties of English.

Until the sixteenth century, the Irish spoke Gaelic, and even today, some of the most characteristically Irish locutions are closely related to that language. "There was me bicycle, leanin' up against the wall stolen," and "Would you be wanting a room for the night, then?" are only two examples.

Gaeltacht is the name given to parts of the country where people

still speak the ancient tongue. These are generally the sparsely populated and beautiful areas on the west coast—Donegal, Mayo, Galway, Kerry—and pockets in the south, near Cork, and in County Waterford and County Meath.

The 1922 Constitution proclaimed Gaelic an official language, and its study was made compulsory in primary schools. There has been a renewed enthusiasm for this native tongue in recent years and it is not uncommon to hear it used when a bit of privacy is wanted. Though the language sounds very different from English, some phrases, such as "Erin Go Bragh" ("Ireland Forever"), are well-known.

TRADITIONAL IRISH CRAFTS

THE CRAFTS INDUSTRY, once a strictly "cottage" trade, has expanded widely, yet in parts of Ireland the real thing can still be found.

Donegal tweed describes the handwoven cloth of County Donegal. It is now produced mostly on power looms.

The distinctive cream-colored Aran sweaters, or fisherman's sweaters made of undyed wool, are still hand-knit by local women on the Aran Islands and sold throughout the country. The stitches and patterns symbolize the natural elements and features in the Aran way of life. Originally the women spun the wool and the men did the knitting, using goose quills for needles. At one time, patterns were specific to a particular family, for the gruesome task of identifying the bodies of drowned sailors.

The superb glasswork manufactured by Waterford is renowned throughout the world. Waterford crystal is still hand-cut by master craftsmen in the oldest and most famous glass factory in Ireland.

Beleek porcelain produces fine, translucent Parian ware and specializes in woven basket pieces and naturalistic flower decorations. Numerous studio potteries in Ireland supply hand-turned and hand-sponged (meaning paint applied by sponge) articles, like those in Connemara. Other traditional crafts include woodwork, lace, linen, and metalwork, such as the well-known Claddagh ring, which shows two hands clasping a heart.

IRISH SPORTS

IN THE PROVINCES, the most popular sports by far are the "national games," administered by the Gaelic Athletic Association, especially Gaelic football. In Dublin, however, "Gaelic" takes a back seat to two other forms of football: rugby and soccer. English soccer teams are considered better skilled than Irish teams, and Dublin soccer fans are primarily interested in English soccer. Since Ireland can offer only limited opportunities in domestic competition, many of the best players go overseas to England.

Hurling is a beloved and distinctly Irish sport, dating back before the Christian era. This fast and furious game resembles field hockey, but the ball can be hit in the air, as well as along the ground, caught in the air, or carried on the flattened end of the player's stick. This stick is called the hurley.

Horse racing is popular throughout Ireland, and the power and grace of Irish thoroughbreds is world-renowned. The best-known courses are the Curragh, Punchestown, Leopardstown, and Fairyhouse in the Dublin area. The Dublin Horse Show, an annual six-day event held in early August, has become the center of the international equestrian world.

The buying and selling of horses in Ireland often follows an ancient ritual. After a potential buyer declares an offer, he spits on his hand and slaps it against the seller's open palm. The offer is bound to be turned down, but with some dramatic gesturing, the help of an enthusiastic crowd, and more spitting and slapping, a price is agreed upon and hands shaken. This old custom says the horse means more to both buyer and seller than the money it can earn.

Gaelic Society's Hurling and Football Grounds, Hicks Estate, Woode

Played Hurling and Football New Jersey, Troy, N.Y., are

MUSIC AND SONG thrive today in Ireland. Every town and village echoes with the sounds of tin whistles and fiddles, while pubs host "sessions," ad-hoc improvisations with local folk musicians.

The harp, Ireland's national symbol, was once widely popular and was commonly used to accompany storytellers. From 1100 to 1600, harpists and poets provided entertainment for the Gaelic chieftains. In the seventeenth and eighteenth centuries, harpists commonly traveled from household to household to entertain. This practice has now declined and much of the intricate technique necessary for learning and playing the harp has been forgotten or lost.

The uillean pipes (elbow pipes) were developed in the seventeenth century and can be made to sound like the human voice. These bagpipes are much more complex than ordinary bagpipes and great skill is needed to play them. Weddings, funerals, and parades are some of the occasions where these special instruments are played.

The fiddle used in traditional Irish music differs from the violin only in the way it

is played. It is often held resting on the shoulder without a chin support; only a small section of the bow is used, and the musician usually plays only the bottom two strings.

The Irish flute is made of wood, and although it has a range of several octaves, usually only the bottom octave is used.

Irish music, especially folk and rock, has become popular throughout the world, as groups like the Clancy Brothers, the Dubliners, and U2, and individual performers like Van Morrison, Enya, and Sinead O'Connor put the Emerald Isle on the charts.

"The Last Rose of Summer" is a traditional Irish ballad: lilting, lyrical, and bittersweet.

'Tis the last rose of summer
Left blooming alone;
All her lovely companions
Are faded and gone;
No flow'r of her kindred,
No rose bud is nigh
To reflect back her blushes,
Or give sigh for sigh!

I'll not leave thee, thou lone one!
To pine on the stem;
Since the lovely are sleeping,
Go, sleep thou with them;
Thus kindly I scatter
Thy leaves o'er the bed,
Where thy mates of the garden
Lie scentless and dead.

So soon may I follow,
When friendships decay,
And from love's shining circle
The gems drop away!
When true hearts lie wither'd,
And fond ones are flown,
Oh! Who would inhabit
This bleak world alone?

IRELAND IS the home of the limerick, named for the Irish port city of the same name, where, it is said, the Irish brigade invented the rhyming verse while returning from France in the eighteenth century.

A ghost in the town of Macroom
One night found a ghoul in his room;
    They argued all night,
    As to who had the right
To frighten the wits out of whom.

☘

There once were two cats of Kilkenny,
Each thought there was one cat too many;
    So they scratched and they bit,
    In a quarrelsome fit,
'Til instead of two cats there weren't any.

☘

There was an old man of Kilbride,
Who slipped in a sewer and died.
    His stupid young brother,
    Went into another,
And the verdict on both was "sewercide."

Proverbs have been passed along by word of mouth for generations.

🍀 A tune is more lasting than the song of birds. And a word is more lasting than the wealth of the world.

🍀 Two shorten the road.

🍀 Three things that are never seen are a blade's edge, the wind, and love.

🍀 The far-off hills are the greenest.

Irish toasts are as gentle and warm as the Irish themselves, and are often tinged with humor.

♣ May you be poor in misfortune,
Rich in blessing,
Slow to make enemies,
Quick to make friends.
But rich or poor, quick or slow,
May you know nothing
But happiness
From this day forth.

♣ May you be in heaven half an hour before the Devil knows you're dead!

♣ May the Leprechauns be near you to spread luck along your way and may all the Irish angels smile upon you on St. Pat's day.

♣ May the road rise up to meet you
And may the wind always be at your back
May the sun shine warm upon your face
And the raindrops fall soft upon your fields
And until we meet again
May God hold you in the small of his hand!

PUB CULTURE

HOSPITALITY is found everywhere in Ireland, but the center of social life in every village and town is the local pub.

Protocol or local custom dictates that when you enter a pub, you greet everyone and take a seat by yourself until invited to join a table. Then the ancient custom of rounds begins, with the newcomer offering to buy the first set of drinks. When the pints are barely half empty, someone else offers a round, and so on, in turn. It can take all afternoon to go around the entire table.

If you're smoking, custom similarly demands that you offer the pack to those with you before you light up.

Women can choose to participate in or be exempted from these rituals. However, in some rural areas, the sight of a woman drinking is still frowned upon, and some pubs have a separate lounge for the ladies.

THE ART OF STORYTELLING

THE IRISH NARRATIVE heritage can be traced back to the Celts who invaded Ireland and brought with them their love of feasting, storytelling, and music. Celtic culture had a long and sophisticated history of storytelling, much in the tradition of the *Iliad*, and the Celts loved to tell their tales of epic battles and supernatural events at firelit feasts. These sagas were passed orally from one generation to the next until someone, most likely a medieval monk, finally wrote them down.

Celtic storytelling thrived in rural Ireland until recently, with a storyteller, or *seanachai*, in every parish. Today the art is dwindling, but some of the most popular stories are widely available in collections of Irish folktales. Nothing can replace the real thing, however, and it is still possible to find an occasional traveling storyteller in a rural pub, spinning together tales of human folly, adventure, and superstition.

Ireland has produced an overabundance of great writers, from Edmund Spenser, the peerless poet and author of *The Faerie Queene*, to Jonathan Swift, the outstanding satirist and author of *Gulliver's Travels*. Laurence Sterne, in *Tristram Shandy* over two hundred years ago, wrote a novel so astonishingly modern that it is at least one hundred years ahead of its time even now. Sheridan LeFanu was a master of the Gothic, a tradition extended by Oscar Wilde, the greatest wit (and one of the greatest playwrights) of his time. John Millington Synge's shattering tragedies soar with the inflections of Ireland, and George Bernard Shaw's comedies are perhaps the most sparkling since the Restoration. James Joyce's *Ulysses* is the quintessential modern novel; Samuel Beckett extended his own austere aesthetic into both prose fiction and theater. And, finally, in William Butler Yeats we have not only perhaps the greatest poet of the century but one in whose every meter beats the Irish soul. This list is far from exhaustive.

W HEN YOU'RE in Ireland, it would be wise to keep an open mind about fairies. As one Irishman put it, "I don't believe in fairies, but they're there."

Leprechauns are the working fairies, the cobblers and tailors. Often in the evening they can be found under a hedge stitching away at a garment or pounding a wee hammer to make a pair of shoes. The Pooka fairy will sometimes help with the housework but can also be very mischievous. The Clobher–Ceann is a naughty fairy who is usually found drinking.

Fairies have been known to carry off small children to raise as their own. These spirits are frightened by fire and iron, however, so remember never to leave a baby alone without taking the proper precautions. Sew a tiny piece of iron into an infant's garment to protect it from bad fairies. Hang an iron horseshoe above your door to protect your home.

Some of the oldest and wealthiest families in Ireland readily admit that they are haunted by spirits. Old manor houses and castles all seem to have their own resident ghosts. Banshees, from the Celtic *bean is*, meaning "woman of the fairies," is the name given to the spirits whose wailing heralds the death of members of aristocratic Irish families, especially those whose surnames are prefixed by O or Mac.

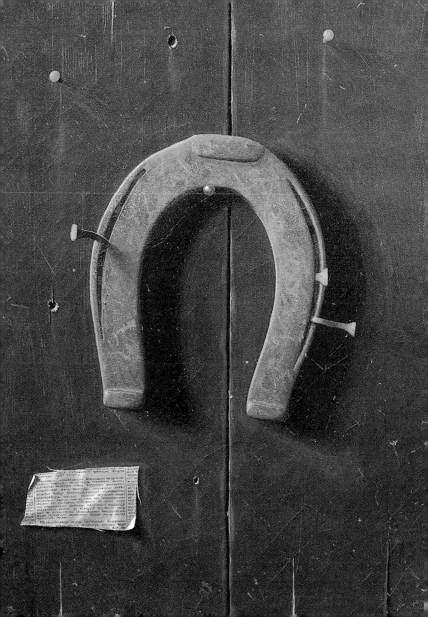

SAINT PATRICK, the patron saint of Ireland, was captured by Irish raiders when he was young and brought from his native France to Ireland as a slave. After six years, he escaped and returned to France. No one knows for certain what brought him back to Ireland, but he returned and dedicated his life to challenging the druids (Celtic priests) and converting the kings of Ireland to Christianity. Some sources say he lived to be 104.

It is believed that he spent forty days and nights in prayer, during which time it rained constantly. Thankful for the bad weather that allowed him to concentrate on his prayers, he banished all poisonous creatures, including snakes, from Ireland.

Until the late seventeenth century the Irish never used "Patrick" as a first name out of respect. Now one in four males is named for the patron saint. Saint Patrick's Day, celebrated on March 17, is a solemn day in Ireland, marked by religious devotion and prayers.

Legend has it that Saint Patrick plucked a shamrock from among the grasses and, holding it up, explained to the crowd how its three leaves were symbolic of the Trinity of Father, Son, and Holy Ghost, three in one. Ever since then, the shamrock has been the symbol of Ireland.

If thou be mine, be mine both day and night,
If thou be mine, be mine in all men's sight,
If thou be mine, be mine o'er all beside—
And oh, that thou wert now my wedded bride.

—EDWARD WALSH, TRANSLATED FROM THE IRISH

♣

Order is an exotic in Ireland. It has been imported from England but it will not grow. It suits neither soil nor climate.

—J. A. FROUDE

♣

In Dublin's fair city
Where the girls are so pretty,
I first set my eyes on sweet Molly Malone,
She wheeled her wheelbarrow
Through streets broad and narrow,
Crying 'Cockles and mussels, alive, alive oh!'

—ANONYMOUS, OLD STREET SONG

In some parts of Ireland, the sleep which knows no waking is always followed by the wake which has no sleeping.

—MARY WILSON LITTLE

♣

Christ with me, Christ before me, Christ behind me,
Christ in me, Christ beneath me, Christ above me,
Christ on my right, Christ on my left,
Christ when I lie down, Christ when I sit down,
    Christ when I arise.
Christ in the heart of every man who thinks of me,
Christ in the mouth of every one who speaks of me,
Christ in every eye that sees me,
Christ in every ear that hears me.

—ANONYMOUS, FROM SAINT PATRICK'S BREASTPLATE,
EIGHTH CENTURY

♣

Wine comes in at the mouth
And love comes in at the eye;
That's all we shall know for truth
Before we grow old and die.
I lift the glass to my mouth,
I look at you, and I sigh.

—W. B. YEATS, "A DRINKING SONG"

She is a rich and rare land;
Oh! she's a fresh and fair land;
She is a dear and rare land—
This native land of mine.

—THOMAS DAVIS, "IRELAND—MY LAND"

♣

When anyone asks me about the Irish character, I say look at the trees. Maimed, stark and misshapen, but ferociously tenacious.

—EDNA O'BRIEN

I'm troubled, I'm dissatisfied. I'm Irish.

—MARIANNE MOORE

♣

What's the use of being Irish if the world doesn't break your heart?

—JOHN F. KENNEDY

♣

So I have come into Wicklow, where the fields are sharply green, where a wild beauty hides in the glens, where sudden surprising vistas open up as the road rises and falls; and here I smell for the first time the incense of Ireland, the smoke of turf fires, and here for the first time I see the face of the Irish countryside.

—H. V. MORTON

♣

Ireland without her people is nothing to me.

—JAMES CONNOLLY

♣

O. Carty

Mona gan

Baron of
Dun: garo.

Lacus Eaug

Armagh Metropolis.

age

eurij

Banne flu.

Shotte

Maßerne

ournele.

Downe

Dun:
rome.

Ca leard

Andeley

Skateryk

Bangor

Sauaige

Newtoun

Argly

ngford hauer.